Seductive Salsa

Rio Nuevo Publishers®

P.O. Box 5250, Tucson, Arizona 85703-0250

(520) 623-9558, www.rionuevo.com

Text and photography © 2006 by Rio Nuevo Publishers. Food styling by Tracy Vega and Carrie Stusse.

Photography credits as follows:
W. Ross Humphreys: front cover, pages 3, 4 right, 5, 16, 29, 37, 53, 77
Robin Stancliff: back cover, pages 4 left, 20, 24, 35, 40, 45, 46, 51, 56, 60, 67, 68, 73, 74.

Library of Congress Cataloging-in-Publication Data

Doland, Gwyneth.
Seductive salsa / Gwyneth Doland.
    p. cm. — (Cook west series)
Includes index.
ISBN 978-1-933855-02-8
1. Salsas (Cookery) I. Title.
TX819.S29D65 2007
641.8'14—dc22

                                    2006102509

Design: Karen Schober, Seattle, Washington.

Printed in Korea.

10   9   8   7   6   5   4   3   2   1

seductive salsa

GWYNETH DOLAND

COOK WEST
SERIES

RIO NUEVO PUBLISHERS
TUCSON, ARIZONA

introduction

Salsa is the Spanish word for "sauce," and although most Americans think of it as that chunky red stuff that comes out of a jar and gets eaten with tortilla chips, in Mexico the word refers to pretty much anything that falls in the broad category of "sauce," including gravy, spaghetti sauce, and chocolate sauce. As far as this book is concerned, salsa is a condiment that usually—but not always—involves chiles, tomatoes or tomatillos, onion, garlic, lime juice, fresh herbs, and salt. It may also include pineapple, jicama, peaches, cucumbers, or black beans. It may be coarsely chopped (like *pico de gallo* or *salsa cruda*), chunky but saucy (like *salsa roja*), or completely smooth (like *salsa verde*). It may be raw or cooked. It's hard to say exactly what's a salsa and what's not, but that's the joy of it. Salsa is a nearly blank canvas, just waiting for your inspiration to strike with bold splashes of flavor.

Salsa does, of course, have its roots firmly planted in the Americas. Chile peppers have been a part of the diet here for more than 7,000 years, and tomatoes were unknown in the rest of the world until European explorers brought them back from the New World. For ages, Mesoamerican cooks have been grinding together chiles and tomatoes in rough stone mortars, and today, salsa is still a part of every meal in Mexico, as common as salt and pepper are in the U.S. Like the chutneys of India or the pickles and relishes of England, this ever-present condiment takes innumerable forms to enliven eggs at breakfast, fish tacos at lunch, and hearty soups at dinner. Every cook has his or her own favorite version, and regional specialties are prized.

Once thought of as an exotic ethnic food, salsa started gaining popularity in the U.S. in the 1980s. Back then, Pace ran a series of commercials mocking any salsa that wasn't from the Southwest, much less from someplace like "New York City!" While most Mexican salsas remain chile-based, American salsas evolved from a more tomato-based formula that appeals to palates unaccustomed to so much fire.

In the past few decades, salsa has become a nationwide household staple, outselling the most American of condiments, ketchup. Now we proudly claim it as our own, enjoying it as part of Mexican meals, but also improvising on the theme and making salsas out of nontraditional ingredients.

TECHNIQUE   The ancient method of making salsa, grinding by hand in a mortar and pestle, still gives the best flavor. Aromatic garlic and pungent chiles release intense flavors as they are ground with a pear-sized *tejolote* in a big *molcajete*. Of course, most Americans have blenders and food processors, not stone mortars, so that's what we're used to using. But if you're serious about salsa, you should seek out this ancient equipment. Molcajetes come in various sizes, but look for one large enough to hold several cups of salsa. Look for them in Mexican markets, or online (see Sources, page 78).

Roasting tomatoes, onions, and chiles brings out another level of flavor that is especially appealing. Don't be tempted to skip over recipes that require these extra steps. I promise you'll be surprised by what a difference it makes. If you want to broil the ingredients instead of roasting them in a cast-iron pan on the stovetop, go ahead. That works just as well, if not better. You could also grill many of the ingredients. Experiment with different methods and use what works for you.

Many recipes call for allowing the salsa to rest. This is an important step, especially in chunky recipes that don't call for pureeing. You may find that a pico de gallo you thought was way too hot at first has mellowed by 30 minutes later, or the salsa that wasn't smoky enough just needed a little time to "get it together." Some cooked and pureed salsas may keep well for several days in the refrigerator, but generally speaking, salsa is prized for its freshness and tastes best the day it's made.

Chiles provide the kick that keeps us addicted to salsa. More and more varieties of chiles show up every day in American supermarkets, and you'll likely find a surprising array of chile peppers for sale at your local farmers market. (See Sources, page 78). Don't be afraid to substitute one chile for another. It may be untraditional, but your experiments will always be interesting (and almost always edible). Just remember to add a little bit at a time.

CHILES

Ají is the generic term used to refer to chiles in South America. There are many varieties of *ají,* but they are often small, yellow or orange, and quite hot. Not very common in grocery stores north of the U.S./Mexico border, they are sometimes found in farmers markets. You can substitute any hot yellow pepper or a small bit of habanero.

Anchos are dried poblano chiles. They are broad-shouldered, with a dark red color and mild, raisiny flavor. They must be rehydrated before being added to a salsa you are planning to puree.

Chile Caribe is the term used to describe crushed red New Mexico chile pods that are often used as a garnish or made into a chile paste. Chile Caribe adds a fruity, medium-hot flavor to salsas.

Chipotle chiles are smoked jalapeños with an intense smoky flavor and sharp heat. They are commonly available canned, in a tomato-based *adobo* sauce. Dried chipotles come in two main varieties: the shiny, dark red variety called *morita*, and a dull, leathery-looking form called *meco*. Use whatever you can get your hands on.

De árbol chiles are skinny little red chiles most often found dried. They are quite hot.

Guajillos are bright red chiles that resemble dried red New Mexico chiles, but their skins are far tougher, and they must be soaked in hot water longer before they soften. They are quite hot, but very flavorful.

Güero chiles, pale yellow fresh chiles with a spicy kick, have become more common lately in grocery stores.

Habanero chiles are known for their intense heat and unusual, fruity, floral flavor. Be very careful when handling habaneros and wear disposable latex gloves or wash your hands thoroughly after handling them. Most of the recipes here call for a quarter of one habanero. I suggest you start with that amount, let the salsa rest, then taste it and add more chile if you like.

Jalapeños are short, dark green, and hot, with a fresh, tart flavor. Pickled jalapeños are slightly milder and are often used as a garnish.

New Mexico red chiles are big, long, dried red chiles. Thin-skinned with a bright, fruity flavor, they are some of the most common red chiles in grocery stores.

Pasillas are long, skinny, dark brown chiles with a medium-hot kick and a rich, complex flavor. They are sometimes called *chiles negros*.

Pequín chiles are tiny (or *pequeño*, in Spanish) but incredibly fiery. They are commonly crushed between the fingers and sprinkled into dishes, but they can also add a pleasant kick to salsa.

Poblanos, the fresh form of anchos, are heart-shaped, dark green chiles with a mild heat. They have a much more complex flavor than green bell pepper and taste wonderful when roasted.

Serranos, native to the mountains north of Puebla, Mexico, are small, dark green chiles that look like skinny jalapeños. Like jalapeños, they are quite hot, with a fresh, citrusy flavor.

Avocados are native to Central America and give many salsas a rich, creamy texture. Choose the smaller, bumpy-surfaced Hass variety over the bland, smooth-skinned Florida avocados, and plan ahead when making guacamole or another avocado salsa, because avocados almost always need a few days to ripen on the counter. (You might be interested to know that avocados hang from the tree in pendulous pairs, earning them the Aztec name *ahuacatl*, or "testicle.")

FRUITS AND VEGETABLES

Cilantro is related to parsley, dill, chervil, and fennel, but it is a much more controversial ingredient than any other herb. The bright, fresh, citrusy flavor is absolutely essential to Mexican and Latin American cuisines. If you hate cilantro, you can certainly exclude it from these recipes, but you'll be missing out. I suggest you add a small amount instead of none at all. If you love it but your friends and family don't, I give the same advice. A light hand with the cilantro will bring you many a convert.

Garlic, like its cousins the onion, leek, shallot, and chive, is a member of the lily family. Mexican garlic has streaks of violet marking its papery bulbs and a somewhat milder flavor than American garlic. Do not buy jars of garlic; the flavor is nothing like fresh. Most chefs don't use garlic presses because they don't save a significant amount of time. Also, many people don't like the mushy texture the presses produce. I say if you're making salsa you're going to be doing a lot of chopping, so you might as well get used to it.

Jicama is the rather dull-looking relative of the sweet potato. But what it lacks in color it makes up for in an exceptionally crunchy texture. The flavor is very mild, in between water chestnut and Asian pear. It is a common ingredient in pico de gallo.

Limes in the U.S. are most often of the Persian variety, but in the rest of the world, what we call Key limes (also sometimes called Mexican limes) are more common. Key limes are smaller but juicier and more acidic than Persian limes, so use them if you can find them, but don't choose bottled Key lime juice (or any packaged lime juice, for that matter) over fresh Persian limes.

Mexican oregano has a stronger flavor than Mediterranean oregano, If you use Mediterranean oregano in your salsa, you may think it tastes like spaghetti sauce. Don't do it. Look for Mexican oregano in the spice aisle or in the Mexican foods section of your grocery store.

Onions. White onions are the standard in Mexico, where they are prized for their clean, sweet, tangy flavor. Yellow onions have a more complex flavor, but they are often too pungent to eat raw. Red onions are not only pretty, but also plenty sweet for eating raw. Green onions add a delicate flavor and interesting texture to a salsa. Rinsing any variety of chopped onion before you add it to an uncooked salsa will make it less pungent.

Tomatillos are related to tomatoes (and also to gooseberries, hence their common papery husks) and are much more popular in Mexico than in the U.S. Known south of the border as *tomates verdes*, they may cause translation problems, but you'll have no problem telling the difference. Tomatillos have a unique tart flavor that is almost like unripe tomatoes, but much brighter and more citrusy. Fresh tomatillos are firm, and their husks are soft and cling to the fruit. Roasting tomatillos mellows their flavor.

Tomatoes. Always let tomatoes ripen on the counter. Never refrigerate them unless they're about to go bad and you need to save them for one more day. In the summer I like to buy every kind of tomato I can find at our local farmers markets. In the winter, I like the little cherry, grape, and pear tomatoes that have become a lot more common lately; they're sweeter than the big tomatoes grocery stores stock out of season. Seeding tomatoes before adding them to a salsa will make the final result less juicy. Roasting them adds a more complex flavor. You can roast tomatoes in a cast-iron skillet, under a broiler, or on a grill.

EQUIPMENT

Blender. A blender works well for pureeing some salsas, especially those that call for dried and rehydrated chiles.

Cast-iron skillet. A large cast-iron skillet, which becomes nonstick with use and age, is very useful for toasting spices, heating tortillas, and frying meats. They are inexpensive, so do yourself a favor and get one.

Food processor. Salsas made without a lot of juicy tomatoes are hard to puree in the blender. The food processor will chop ingredients no matter how much liquid is in the workbowl. It also gives you more control over a range of textures from smooth to chunky.

Lime/lemon press. Made from cast aluminum (sometimes polished and sometimes powder-coated), and resembling a giant garlic press, this is the best tool for squeezing juice from lemons and limes. It's better than a reamer and superior to most inexpensive juicers.

Molcajete y tejolote. The Mexican version of a mortar (*molcajete*) and pestle (*tejolote*) is carved out of heavy lava rock. (See page 45 for a picture of a molcajete that is being used as a serving dish.) This is the most traditional tool for making salsa, and it produces a result that is impossible to achieve with a machine. The mortar roughs out smooth edges on the ingredients while maintaining a chunky texture.

Grinding garlic, chiles, and tomatoes in a big mortar requires a little elbow grease, but it's fun, your friends will get a kick out of it, and the resulting salsa will taste great. Buy one that's big enough to hold several cups of salsa; it is well worth the investment ($25 to $50).

Traditional Salsas

xxxxxx

Salsa Roja de Molcajete

xxxxxx

*Impress your guests by making this traditional red salsa with a big lava-rock mortar and pestle (*molcajete *and* tejolote*). If you don't have one, put the ingredients in the work bowl of your food processor and pulse until it is smooth but still chunky. Serve the salsa in the* molcajete, *with freshly fried tortilla chips.*

Using the *tejolote*, grind the garlic to a paste in the *molcajete*. Add the onion and chiles and grind until blended. Add the tomatoes, crushing and grinding until smooth but still chunky. Season to taste with salt.

Makes about 1½ cups

2 cloves garlic

¼ cup chopped white onion

1–2 jalapeño chiles, stemmed, seeded, and chopped

3 medium tomatoes, chopped and seeded

Salt

Salsa Verde de Molcajete

xxxxxx

The uncooked tomatillos in this green salsa give it a refreshing tart flavor.

Using the *tejolote*, grind the garlic to a paste in the *molcajete*. Add the onion and chiles and grind until blended. Add the tomatillos, crushing and grinding until smooth but still chunky. Stir in the cilantro and season to taste with salt. If you don't have a *molcajete*, put the ingredients in the workbowl of your food processor and pulse until it is smooth but still chunky. Serve the salsa in the *molcajete*, with freshly fried tortilla chips.

Makes about 2 cups

2 cloves garlic

¼ cup chopped white onion

2 jalapeño chiles, stemmed, seeded, and chopped

½ pound tomatillos, husked and chopped

2 tablespoons chopped cilantro leaves

Salt

Guacamole de Molcajete

xxxxxx

Makes about 2 cups

2 cloves garlic

2 tablespoons chopped white onion

2 jalapeños, stemmed, seeded, and chopped

2 large, ripe avocados, peeled, pitted, and roughly chopped

1 medium tomato, seeded and diced

1/4 cup chopped cilantro leaves

Juice of 1 lime, or to taste

Salt

As you know, avocados quickly turn brown after they're cut, so guacamole starts to look pretty yucky if you make it too far in advance. The best way to prepare and serve this traditional Mexican appetizer is to let your guests watch you grind up the ingredients in the molcajete *and then serve it straight from the bowl of the mortar.*

Using the *tejolote*, grind the garlic to a paste in the *molcajete*. Add the onion and jalapeños and grind until blended. Add the avocados, crushing just until blended. Stir in the tomato, cilantro, and lime juice. Season to taste with salt and serve immediately.

Salsa Mexicana I

xxxxxx

Makes 4 cups

4 medium tomatoes, seeded and diced

1 small Vidalia or other variety of sweet onion, diced

1 clove garlic, minced

1 jalapeño chile, stemmed, seeded, and minced

2 tablespoons chopped cilantro leaves

Juice of 2 limes, or to taste

Salt

I created this recipe one summer evening when I was on vacation with extended family at the beach in North Carolina. I wanted to create a garnish that I was sure the kids would eat, so this very basic salsa is heavy on the tomatoes and light on the chiles, with just a hint of cilantro. Everyone liked it, including my uncle who absolutely hates *cilantro, and the kids were interested to learn that the red, white, and green colors of the salsa represent the colors of the Mexican flag.*

In a bowl, toss together the tomatoes, onion, garlic, jalapeño, and cilantro. Season to taste with lime juice and salt.

Salsa Mexicana II

xxxxxx

Once you've convinced your crowd that homemade salsa is good and a little jalapeño won't kill them, you can spice it up a little bit.

In a bowl, toss together the tomatoes, onion, garlic, jalapeño, and cilantro. Season to taste with lime juice and salt.

Makes 4 cups

4 medium tomatoes, seeded and diced

1 small white onion, diced

2 cloves garlic, minced

3–5 jalapeño chiles, stemmed, seeded, and minced

$1/4$ cup chopped cilantro leaves

Juice of 2 limes, or to taste

Salt

Quick Salsa Roja

xxxxxx

Most canned tomatoes are disappointing, but the "fire roasted" tomatoes (such as Muir Glen brand) work well for this quick salsa that's great for dipping with chips.

Heat the lard or oil in a heavy-bottomed saucepan over medium heat and add the onion, garlic, jalapeños, and tomatoes. Fry the mixture, stirring constantly for 5–10 minutes, until the sauce has thickened. Season to taste with salt.

Makes about 2½ cups

1 tablespoon lard or vegetable oil

$1/2$ cup diced white onion

1 clove garlic, minced

2 jalapeño chiles, stemmed, seeded, and minced

1 can (15 ounces) crushed "fire-roasted" tomatoes

Salt

Roasted Tomatillo Salsa

xxxxxx

Pan-roasting the ingredients for this salsa gives it a rich, mellow flavor. Serve it at room temperature with tortilla chips, or warmed and spooned over any grilled meat.

In a cast-iron skillet over medium heat, roast the tomatillos, allowing them to char a little on each side and shaking the pan occasionally to redistribute them. Transfer the tomatillos to a plate to cool.

Add the garlic, onion rings, and jalapeños to the pan and cook, allowing the skin of the chiles to darken and blister, and the onions to char a little on each side. The garlic should pick up some golden patches. Transfer the chiles, onion, and garlic to a cutting board.

Remove their papery husks and roughly chop the tomatillos; add them to the workbowl of your food processor.

Peel the garlic cloves and roughly chop them and the onion slices. Stem, seed, and chop the chiles. Transfer the garlic, onions, and chiles to the food processor and pulse until smooth, adding water if the salsa is too thick.

Pour the puree into a bowl, stir in the cilantro, and season to taste with salt.

Makes about 2 cups

$1/2$ **pound tomatillos**

2 cloves garlic, unpeeled

$1/2$ **medium white onion, sliced into rings 1 inch thick**

2 jalapeño chiles

$1/4$ **cup water, if needed**

$1/3$ **cup finely chopped cilantro leaves**

Salt

Tomatillo Avocado Salsa

xxxxxx

Makes about 3 cups

1/2 **pound tomatillos**

2 **cloves garlic, unpeeled**

1/2 **medium white onion, sliced into rings 1 inch thick**

2 **serrano chiles**

1 **medium avocado, peeled, pitted, and diced**

1/3 **cup finely chopped cilantro leaves**

Juice of 1 lime

Salt

The addition of avocado doesn't make this a guacamole, but it does mellow out the tart tomatillos. The lime juice keeps the dish tangy. Serve this salsa at room temperature with tortilla chips, or warmed and spooned over any grilled meat.

In a cast-iron skillet over medium heat, roast the tomatillos, allowing them to char a little on each side and shaking the pan occasionally to redistribute them. Transfer the tomatillos to a plate to cool.

Add the garlic, onion rings, and chiles to the pan and cook, allowing the skin of the chiles to darken and blister, and the onions to char a little on each side. The garlic should start to pick up some golden patches. Transfer the chiles, onion, and garlic to a cutting board.

Remove their papery husks and roughly chop the tomatillos; add them to the workbowl of your food processor.

Peel the garlic cloves and roughly chop them and the onion slices. Stem, seed, and chop the chiles. Transfer the garlic, onions, chiles, and avocado to the food processor and pulse until smooth.

Pour the puree into a bowl, stir in the cilantro and lime juice, and season to taste with salt.

Everyday Pico de Gallo

xxxxxx

Pico de gallo *means "rooster's beak" in Spanish, and the name refers to the pecking motion of your fingers as you pinch a little bit of the salsa from the bowl to sprinkle on your tacos. This traditional fresh salsa goes well with almost anything. Use it to top eggs, steaks, and tacos, or simply serve it with tortilla chips. For more variations on this theme, see the "Pico de Gallo and Other Chunky Salsas" section.*

In a bowl, toss the tomatoes with the garlic, onion, jalapeños, and cilantro. Season to taste with lime juice and salt. Allow the mixture to sit at room temperature for about 30 minutes to let the flavors fully develop.

Makes about 3 cups

1 pound tomatoes, seeded and diced

1 garlic clove, minced

1 small onion, chopped

2 jalapeños, stemmed, seeded, and minced

1/4 cup chopped cilantro

Juice of 1–2 limes

Salt

Fiery Chile Salsas
xxxxxx

Fiery Peanut Salsa

xxxxxx

This rich, intense salsa comes from Veracruz, Mexico. Use it as a dip for grilled chicken skewers or pour it over thick slices of grilled pork tenderloin. Use peanuts that are dry-roasted but unsalted.

Heat the peanut oil in a cast-iron skillet over medium heat. Sauté the onion and garlic until the onion is softened and the garlic is golden. Add the tomatoes and chiles to the pan and cook 10–15 minutes, or until the tomatoes release their juices and thicken.

Transfer the mixture to the blender, add the peanuts, and puree until smooth. Add a little water to thin the sauce, if desired. Season to taste with salt, garnish with a few more chopped peanuts, and serve.

Makes about 2 cups

1 tablespoon peanut oil

1/4 cup diced white onion

1 garlic clove, chopped

5 medium tomatoes, chopped and seeded

2 chipotle chiles in adobo, chopped

1/4 cup chopped peanuts, plus more for garnish

Salt

Salsa Picante de Chile de Árbol

xxxxxx

Makes about 1½ cups

2 cups water

20 chiles de árbol, stemmed and seeded

2 cloves garlic, minced

2 medium tomatoes

2 tablespoons vinegar

½ teaspoon Mexican oregano

Salt

Sugar

De árbol chiles are fairly short, skinny dried red chiles that are hotter than jalapeños or serranos. Use this smooth salsa when you want a big burst of chile flavor.

In a saucepan over high heat, bring the water to a boil.

Meanwhile, in a cast-iron skillet over medium heat, toast the chiles until they soften and darken, but be careful not to burn them. Transfer the chiles to a medium-sized, heat-safe bowl and pour in enough boiling water to cover. Keep the chiles submerged with a small plate or saucer.

Add the garlic cloves and tomatoes to the skillet and cook, shaking the pan occasionally, until the garlic gathers some golden patches and the tomatoes are mostly charred. Remove the garlic and tomatoes to a cutting board to cool, then mince the garlic and roughly chop the tomatoes.

Using a slotted spoon, remove the chiles from the soaking water and put them in a blender. Reserve the soaking water.

Add the garlic, tomatoes, vinegar, and oregano to the blender and process until smooth, adding a little of the reserved soaking water if necessary. Season to taste with salt and a little bit of sugar.

Salsa Ranchera

xxxxxx

In many parts of the Southwest, this is what you'll find slathered all over huevos rancheros.

In a cast-iron skillet over medium heat, cook the tomatoes for a few minutes, allowing them to char a little on each side. Transfer the tomatoes to a cutting board.

Add the onion rings, garlic, and jalapeños to the pan and cook, allowing the skin of the chiles to darken and blister, and the onions to char a little on each side. The garlic should start to pick up some golden patches. Transfer the chiles, onions, and garlic to a cutting board.

Chop the tomatoes and place them in a blender.

Peel the garlic cloves and roughly chop them and the onion slices. Stem, seed, and chop the chiles. Transfer the garlic, onions, and chiles to the blender and pulse until smooth. Season to taste with salt.

Heat the vegetable oil in a cast-iron skillet over medium heat and fry the puree until thickened slightly, about 10 minutes. Serve hot.

Makes 1½ cups

2 medium tomatoes

½ small white onion, sliced into rings 1 inch thick

1 garlic clove, unpeeled

2 jalapeño chiles

Salt

2 teaspoons vegetable oil

Yucatecan Habanero Salsa

xxxxxx

Makes about 2 cups

1–2 habanero chiles,
stemmed, halved,
and seeded

4 medium tomatoes

1/4 white onion

1/2 teaspoon Mexican
oregano

2 tablespoons
vegetable oil

Salt

Serve this smooth, searing-hot salsa over plump chiles rellenos or tamales steamed in banana leaves.

Place the chiles, whole tomatoes, and onion quarter on a cookie sheet and broil until the tomato skins are blackened. Remove the tomatoes, transfer them to a plate to cool, and continue broiling the chiles and onions until the chile skins are partially blackened. Remove the chiles and onion from the broiler and allow them to cool. Roughly chop the onion.

Remove the tomato skins and transfer the tomatoes to the blender. Add the chiles, chopped onion, and oregano to the workbowl and process until smooth.

Heat the oil in the skillet and fry the sauce for about 5 minutes. Season to taste with salt.

Smoky Chipotle Salsa

xxxxxx

Makes about 2 cups

2 cups water

2 ancho chiles,
stemmed and seeded

4 dried chipotle chiles

4 cloves garlic, unpeeled

3 medium tomatoes

2 tablespoons lard
or vegetable oil

Salt

I love the smoky flavor of chipotles, but I agree with Diana Kennedy, the great champion of Mexican cuisine, when she argues in My Mexico *that a salsa made using only dried chipotles is simply too hot. Here I've taken her suggestion to supplement the chipotles with anchos, but I also added tomatoes to mellow it even further.*

In a saucepan over high heat, bring the water to a boil.

Meanwhile, in a cast-iron skillet over medium heat, toast the ancho and chipotle chiles on both sides until they soften and darken, but be careful not to burn them. Transfer the chiles to a medium-sized, heat-safe bowl and pour in enough boiling water to cover. Keep the chiles submerged with a small plate or saucer.

Add the garlic and tomatoes to the skillet and cook until the garlic gathers some golden patches and the tomatoes are covered with dark splotches. Transfer the tomatoes and garlic to a cutting board to cool. Peel and mince the garlic, then roughly chop the tomatoes.

Using a slotted spoon, remove the chiles from the soaking water and transfer them to a blender. Reserve the soaking water.

Add the tomatoes and garlic to the blender and process until smooth.

Heat the lard or oil in a heavy-bottomed saucepan over medium heat, then add the puree and fry, stirring constantly for 5–10 minutes, until the sauce has thickened. Season to taste with salt.

Salsa Borracha

xxxxxx

This smooth chile salsa is made with tequila, hence the name, which translates to "drunken sauce." Slather this salsa liberally over grilled steak or vegetables.

Makes about 1 cup

¹/₂ **cup vegetable oil**

8 dried pasilla, guajillo, or red New Mexican chiles, stemmed and seeded

1 medium white onion, peeled and diced

1 cup orange juice

¹/₃ **cup tequila**

Heat the vegetable oil in a cast-iron skillet over medium heat. Add the chiles and fry for about 5 minutes, turning often. Using tongs, remove the chiles from the oil and allow them to drain on a paper towel-lined plate.

Pour off the oil, then add the onion to the pan and fry until softened and translucent.

Transfer the onion and chiles to the blender and add the orange juice. Blend until smooth.

Return the pureed sauce and the onion to the skillet and cook over high heat for about 3 minutes, or until the sauce thickens slightly. Remove from heat and stir in the tequila.

New Mexico Red Chile Salsa

xxxxxx

Makes about 1½ cups

2 cups water

4 dried red New Mexico chiles, stemmed and seeded

2 medium tomatoes

½ small white onion, sliced into rings 1 inch thick

3 cloves garlic

½ teaspoon Mexican oregano

1 tablespoon white wine vinegar

Salt

This smooth salsa has the mellow heat and fruity flavor of New Mexico's famous red chiles. Serve it with chips or spooned over tacos.

In a saucepan over high heat, bring the water to a boil.

Meanwhile, in a cast-iron skillet over medium heat, toast the chiles on both sides until they soften and darken, but be careful not to burn them. Transfer the chiles to a medium-sized, heat-safe bowl and pour in enough boiling water to cover. Keep the chiles submerged with a small plate or saucer.

Add the tomatoes, onion rings, and garlic to the skillet and cook until the onions char a little, the garlic gathers some golden patches, and the tomatoes are covered with dark splotches. Transfer the tomatoes, onion, and garlic to a cutting board to cool.

Using a slotted spoon, remove the chiles from the soaking water and put them in a blender. Reserve the soaking water.

Add the tomatoes, onion, garlic, oregano, and vinegar to the blender and process until smooth, adding a little of the reserved soaking water if necessary. Season to taste with salt.

Salsa de Ají Amarillo

xxxxxx

Although ají amarillo *is rare in American markets, many gardeners grow varieties of these South American chiles. If you can't find them, substitute any hot yellow banana or wax pepper; you can also use some yellow bell pepper and a bit of habanero.*

Put the tomatoes, onion, chiles, and cilantro in the workbowl of your food processor and puree until smooth, adding up to ½ cup of water if necessary. Season to taste with salt and serve.

Makes about 2 cups

2 large tomatoes, quartered

1 small white onion, roughly chopped

4 large aji chiles, stemmed, seeded, and chopped

1 tablespoon chopped fresh cilantro leaves

Water

Salt

Pasilla Salsa

xxxxxx

Makes about 1½ cups

2 cups water

3 pasilla chiles, stemmed and seeded

3 cloves garlic

1 small white onion

1 tablespoon lard or vegetable oil

Salt

The rich, deep flavor of this salsa is addictive, especially poured over grilled beef or pork.

In a saucepan over high heat, bring the water to a boil.

Meanwhile, in a cast-iron skillet over medium heat, toast the chiles on both sides until they soften and darken, but be careful not to burn them. Transfer the chiles to a medium-sized, heat-safe bowl and pour in enough boiling water to cover. Keep the chiles submerged with a small plate or saucer.

Add the garlic and onion to the skillet and cook until the garlic gathers some golden patches and the onion is softened and slightly charred. Peel and mince the garlic; roughly chop the onion.

Using a slotted spoon, remove the chiles from the soaking water and add them to the blender. Reserve the soaking water.

Add the garlic and onion to the blender and puree until smooth, adding about 1 cup of the soaking water.

Heat the lard or oil in a heavy-bottomed saucepan over medium heat, then add the puree and fry, stirring constantly for 5–10 minutes, until the sauce has thickened. Season to taste with salt.

Salsa de Chile Pequín

XXXXXX

Makes about 1½ cups

Very easy to make and pretty darn hot.

1 cup water
10 pequín chiles
2 medium tomatoes
5 tomatillos
1 tablespoon chopped cilantro
Salt

In a saucepan over high heat, bring the water to a boil.

Meanwhile, in a cast-iron skillet over medium heat, toast the chiles until they soften and darken, but be careful not to burn them. Transfer the chiles to a medium-sized, heat-safe bowl and pour in enough boiling water to cover. Keep the chiles submerged with a small plate or saucer.

Add the tomatoes and tomatillos and cook until the tomatoes are covered with dark splotches. Transfer the tomatoes and tomatillos to a cutting board to cool.

Using a slotted spoon, remove the chiles from the soaking water and add them to the blender. Reserve the soaking water.

Add the tomatoes, tomatillos, and cilantro to the blender and puree until smooth, adding a little of the reserved soaking water if necessary. Season to taste with salt.

Pico de Gallo and Other Chunky Salsas

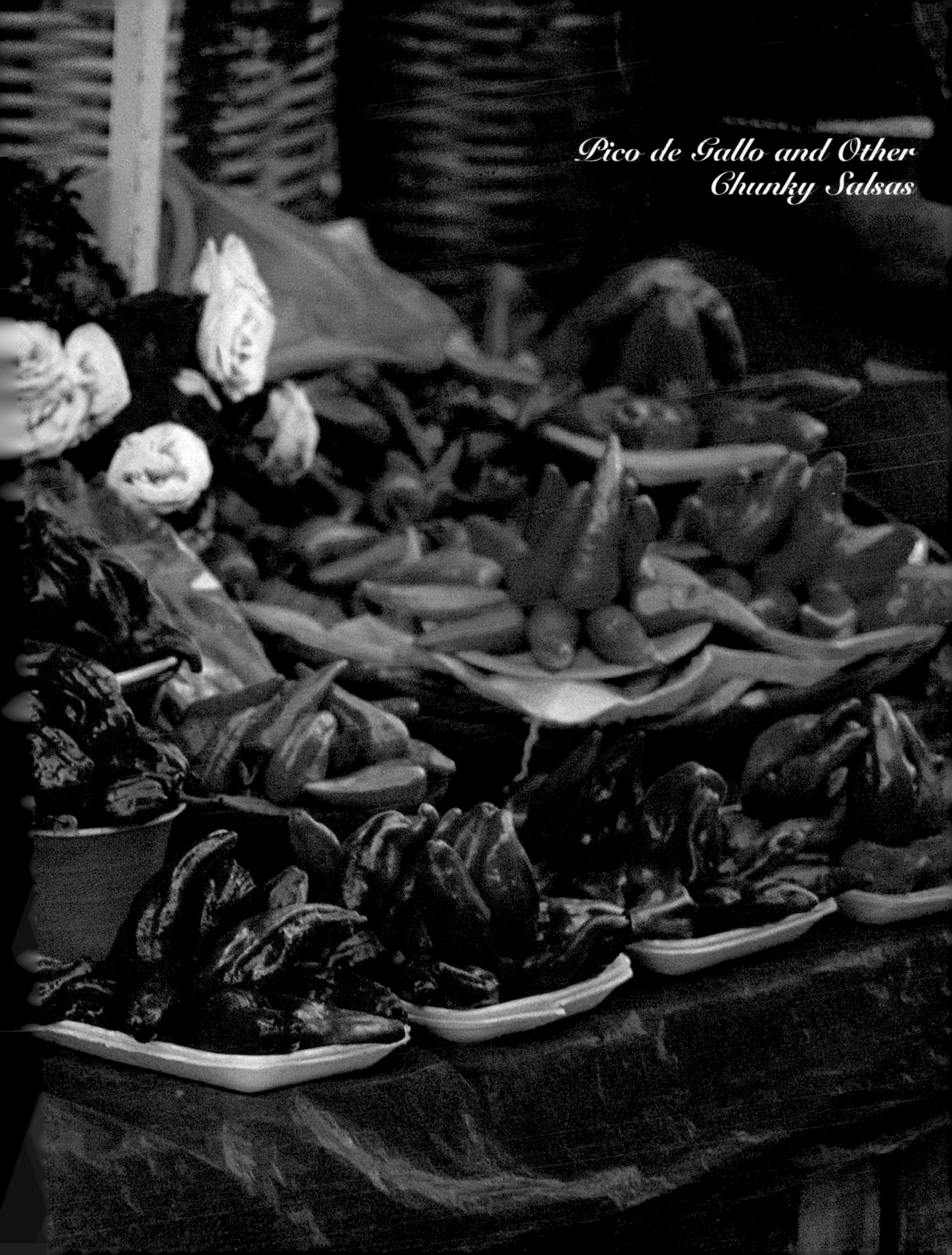

Avocado Pico de Gallo

xxxxx

Makes about 3 cups

2 medium tomatoes,
seeded and diced

1 clove garlic, minced

1 small white onion, diced

2 jalapeño chiles, stemmed,
seeded, and minced

1 small avocado,
peeled, pitted, and diced

Juice of 1 lime

2 tablespoons chopped
cilantro leaves

Salt

This is not guacamole; it's a chunky pico de gallo with a bit of rich, creamy avocado. You can eat it with chips, but it's ideal spooned over tacos or inside an omelet.

In a bowl, toss the tomatoes with the garlic, onion, jalapeños, avocado, and lime juice. Add the cilantro, season to taste with salt, and serve immediately.

Roasted Green Tomato Salsa Verde

xxxxxx

At the end of the summer and into the fall, many gardeners find their tomato plants still laden with green tomatoes that won't have enough time to ripen before the first frost. Most famous when deep-fried, the mild, slightly tart green tomatoes also make a salsa verde *(green salsa) that will appeal especially to people who don't like the much stronger flavor of tomatillos. People who don't care for cilantro should try this recipe with the optional Mexican oregano.*

In a cast-iron skillet over medium heat, cook the tomatoes for a few minutes, allowing them to char a little on each side. Transfer the tomatoes to a cutting board.

Add the garlic, onion rings, and chile to the pan and cook, allowing the skin of the chile to darken and blister, and the onion rings to char a little on each side. The garlic should start to pick up some golden patches. Transfer the chile, onion, and garlic to a cutting board.

Chop the green tomatoes and add them to the workbowl of your food processor.

Peel the garlic cloves and roughly chop them and the onion slices. Transfer the garlic, onions, chile, and Mexican oregano (if using) to the food processor and pulse until smooth, adding the water if the salsa is too thick.

Pour the puree into a bowl, stir in the cilantro (if using), and season to taste with salt.

Makes about 2 cups

3 medium green tomatoes, sliced into rings 1 inch thick

2 cloves garlic, unpeeled

$^1/_2$ medium white onion, sliced into rings 1 inch thick

1 jalapeño chile, stemmed, seeded, and minced

$^1/_4$ cup water (if needed)

$^1/_4$ cup chopped cilantro leaves or 2 teaspoons dried Mexican oregano (optional)

Salt

Herbed Pear Tomato Salsa Fresca

xxxxxx

Delightfully sweet little pear tomatoes are becoming more and more common at farmers markets and well-stocked grocery stores. You can also use grape, currant, or cherry tomatoes for this chunky salsa. Try it on top of grilled slices of rustic bread.

In a bowl, toss the tomatoes with the green onions, garlic, habanero, cilantro, basil, olive oil, and lime juice. Add salt to taste, then let the salsa rest 30 minutes. Adjust the seasonings and serve.

Makes about 2 cups

1 pint yellow pear tomatoes, halved

2 green onions, thinly sliced

1 clove garlic, minced

$1/4$ habanero pepper, stemmed, seeded, and minced

1 tablespoon chopped cilantro leaves

1 tablespoon chopped basil

1 tablespoon extra-virgin olive oil

Juice of 1 lime

Salt

Argentine Chimichurri

xxxxxx

Makes about 2 cups

8 cloves garlic, minced

1/2 cup minced Italian (flat-leaf) parsley

1 tablespoon chile Caribe or any other variety of crushed red pepper flakes

1/4 cup red wine vinegar

1 cup extra-virgin olive oil

Salt and freshly ground black pepper

Chimichurri is to Argentina as ketchup is to America. It is on every table and is the primary marinade and sauce for the country's famous grilled beef. Experiment with using cilantro or fresh oregano instead of parsley and hotter chiles in place of the chile Caribe.

In a bowl, use a whisk to stir together the garlic, parsley, chile flakes, and vinegar. Whisk vigorously as you pour the olive oil into the bowl in a thin stream. Add salt and pepper to taste, then cover and set aside for at least 1 hour.

Pickled Jalapeño Salsa

xxxxxx

Makes about 2 cups

1 tablespoon vegetable oil

1/4 cup diced onion

2 cloves garlic, minced

3 pickled jalapeños, minced

3 medium tomatoes, chopped

1 teaspoon Mexican oregano

Salt

Pickled jalapeños are a bit milder than the fresh ones, with a tangy bite.

Add the vegetable oil to a heavy-bottomed saucepan over low heat. Add the onion and garlic and cook slowly until the onion is translucent. Add the jalapeños, tomatoes, and oregano, and simmer about 5 minutes. Allow the mixture to cool, then add salt to taste. If it's not hot enough, add a little juice from the jar of pickled jalapeños.

Three Green Chile Salsa Cruda

xxxxxx

Salsa cruda is an uncooked salsa with a chunky texture. The bright flavor of green chiles is what stands out in this chip-dipper.

In a bowl, toss together the serrano, jalapeño, and poblano chiles with the onions, tomatoes, cilantro, and avocado. Season to taste with salt and lime juice.

Makes 2 cups

1 serrano chile, seeded and finely diced

2 jalapeño chiles, stemmed, seeded, and minced

1 large poblano chile, seeded and diced

4 green onions, white and green parts, thinly sliced

3 medium tomatoes, cored and diced

$1/4$ cup chopped cilantro leaves

1 medium avocado, peeled and diced

Salt

Juice of 1 lime

Salsa Güera

xxxxxx

Makes about 2 cups

¹/₂ **pound fresh yellow chiles, stemmed, seeded, and finely diced**

¹/₂ **medium white onion, finely chopped**

2 cloves garlic, minced

Juice of 1 lime

Salt

In Spanish, güera *means "blonde," and in Mexico the term is used to refer to several different kinds of pale yellow chiles; use whatever kind of fresh yellow chiles you can find for this recipe. If the chiles are too hot, add a little diced yellow bell pepper; if they aren't hot enough, add a little bit of habanero, serrano, or jalapeño. This sweet/hot salsa tastes great spooned over fish tacos. Notice that the Salsa Güera shown in the picture is served in an authentic molcajete.*

In a bowl, toss the chiles with the onion, garlic, and lime juice. Season to taste with salt.

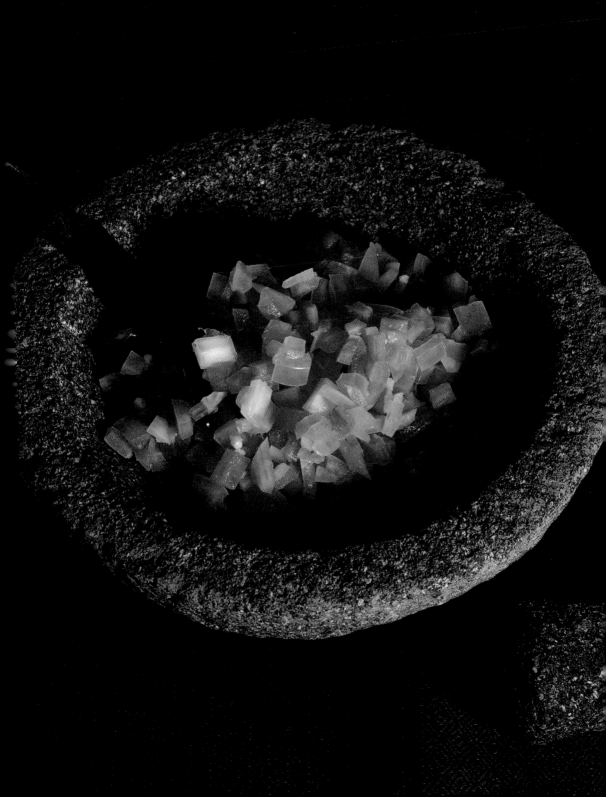

Cactus Paddle and Jicama Salsa Fresca

xxxxxx

The paddles of the prickly pear cactus are called nopales; *when cut into strips for cooking, they're called* nopalitos. *You may find whole paddles or bags of precut strips in the produce section of your market, especially in the spring and summer; also look for them in jars in the Mexican foods section.*

If you're using a whole cactus paddle, carefully remove all of the spines by holding the paddle firmly with tongs while cutting off the spines with a vegetable peeler. Slice the spine-free paddle into *nopalito* strips, each about the size of a skinny green bean.

In a saucepan, bring 1 quart of salted water to a boil. Add the nopalitos and simmer 15 minutes, or until tender. Drain, rinse in cold water, and allow to cool completely, then dice the nopalitos.

In a bowl, toss the diced cactus with the jicama, tomatoes, jalapeños, garlic, onion, cilantro, and lime juice. Season to taste with salt.

Makes about 3 cups

1 large cactus paddle or about 1 cup drained nopalitos from a jar

1/2 cup diced jicama

2 medium tomatoes, seeded and diced

2 jalapeño chiles, stemmed, seeded, and minced

2 cloves garlic, minced

1/2 white onion, diced

1/4 cup chopped cilantro leaves

Juice of 1 lime

Salt

Heirloom Tomato Pico de Gallo

xxxxxx

Makes about 2½ cups

2 cups diced tomatoes in mixed colors

2 jalapeño chiles, stemmed, seeded, and minced

½ cup diced red onion

¼ cup cilantro leaves

Juice of 1 lime

Salt

Make this salsa in the late summer when you can find red, yellow, orange, and green tomatoes at farmers markets. Well-stocked grocery stores and natural food stores also often carry many heirloom varieties, although locally grown tomatoes always taste best. Try this salsa sprinkled over fajitas, chicken tacos, or tuna steaks.

In a bowl, toss the tomatoes with the chiles, onion, cilantro, and lime juice. Season to taste with salt and serve immediately.

Salsa Criolla

xxxxxx

Makes about 2½ cups

2 cloves garlic, minced

¼ cup chopped Italian (flat-leaf) parsley

1 white onion, finely diced

1 red bell pepper, finely diced

1 green, yellow, or orange bell pepper, finely diced

1 medium tomato, seeded and finely diced

¼ cup red wine vinegar

½ cup extra-virgin olive oil

Salt and freshly ground black pepper

Along with chimichurri, this "Creole sauce" is a staple condiment for Argentine meats. Experiment using cilantro, rosemary, or oregano in place of some or all of the parsley.

In a bowl, toss together the garlic, parsley, onion, bell peppers, tomato, and vinegar. Whisk vigorously as you pour the olive oil into the bowl in a thin stream. Add salt and black pepper to taste and serve immediately.

Corn, Squash, and Chile Salsa

xxxxxx

In New Mexico, we make a dish called calabacitas *with summer squash, corn, and green chiles. It is spectacular served over a thick, juicy steak. The proportions of corn, squash, and chiles aren't particularly important, so feel free to improvise.*

Over the flame of your gas grill, stovetop, or broiler, blacken the skin of the poblano. Place it in a large bowl and cover with plastic wrap for 15 minutes (the steam will help loosen the skin). Remove all of the blackened skin from the chile by gently brushing it with your flattened palm. Rinse your hand with cool water from the faucet after every few strokes. Coarsely chop the chile.

Stand the corncob upright on a cutting board and slice off the kernels. Run your knife down the cob afterward to scrape out all of the little milky bits.

In a large skillet over medium heat, melt the lard, bacon grease, or oil. Add the onion and cook until softened. Add the squash and garlic, and stir to combine. Cook, covered, about 10 minutes. Add the corn and chile and continue cooking, uncovered, until the squash is tender. Season to taste with salt and pepper.

Makes about 2½ cups

1 poblano chile

1 large ear fresh corn
(or ³/₄ cup canned corn)

2 tablespoons lard, bacon grease, or vegetable oil

½ small white onion, peeled and diced

1 medium zucchini or other summer squash, diced

2 cloves garlic

Salt and pepper

Confetti Dill Salsa

xxxxxx

Makes about 2 cups

1/2 red bell pepper, finely diced

1/2 yellow bell pepper, finely diced

1/2 orange bell pepper, finely diced

1–3 serrano chiles, finely diced

2 shallots, finely diced

2 tablespoons chopped fresh dill

Juice of 1 lime or lemon

Salt

This salsa is prettiest when you dice everything into ¼-inch-square pieces. It takes time, but people will appreciate it! Serve the salsa with chips or sprinkled over cooked fish, or mix it with a little olive oil and some canned tuna for a colorful tuna salad.

In a bowl, toss together the red, yellow, and orange bell peppers, serrano chiles, shallots, and dill. Season to taste with lime or lemon juice and salt.

East Indian Black-Eyed Pea Salsa

xxxxxx

Makes about 3 cups

1 can (15 ounces) black-eyed peas, rinsed and drained

1 tomato, seeded and diced

1/2 red onion, diced

2 cloves garlic, minced

2 tablespoons chopped cilantro leaves

1 tablespoon grated fresh ginger root

2 teaspoons freshly ground cumin seed

1 teaspoon ground turmeric

1/2 teaspoon ground cardamom

1/4 teaspoon cayenne pepper

Salt

This heavily spiced but not-too-hot salsa can also be served chilled as a side dish, or heated through and served over hot basmati rice.

In a bowl, toss the black-eyed peas with the tomato, onion, garlic, cilantro, ginger, cumin, turmeric, and cardamom. Add cayenne pepper and salt to taste.

Fresh Corn Salsa

xxxxxx

Makes about 2 cups

2 cooked, cooled, and
shucked corncobs

1 medium tomato,
finely diced

1/2 small red onion,
finely chopped

1 jalapeño chile, stemmed,
seeded, and minced

2 tablespoons minced
cilantro, basil, or tarragon

Juice of 1 lime

Salt

I often overestimate the amount of fresh corn to buy when I have a backyard barbecue. I know people like corn, but I think they're hesitant to eat it at parties because they don't want to walk around with big pieces of corn stuck in their teeth. Their loss. I like to make this salsa with the leftovers.

Stand a corncob upright on a cutting board and slice off the kernels. Run your knife down the cob afterward to scrape out all of the little milky bits. Repeat with the other cob and transfer the corn to a medium bowl.

Toss the corn with the tomato, onion, jalapeño, cilantro, and lime juice. Season to taste with salt.

Vietnamese Pickled Carrot and Daikon

xxxxx

This garnish is part of nearly every Vietnamese meal, taking the same place as chunky fresh salsas in Mexican cuisine. The sweet and salty flavor accents everything from noodle bowls to grilled meat and rice dishes and spring rolls. It is an essential ingredient in Vietnamese sandwiches, which also include some kind of meat (cold sliced pork, pâté, bologna, or grilled pork), sliced jalapeños, and cilantro sprigs.

Makes about 2 cups

1 medium carrot

1 daikon radish

$^1/_2$ cup rice vinegar

3 tablespoons sugar

1 teaspoon salt

Peel the carrot and daikon and cut them into very thin matchsticks. (If you have a mandoline, this is the time to use it.) In a bowl, toss the matchsticks with the rice vinegar, sugar, and salt. Marinate at least 1 hour. Taste, adjust seasonings, and pour off any extra liquid before serving.

Bocconcini Salsa

xxxxx

You can make a salad with thick rounds of fresh tomatoes and fresh mozzarella, or you can make a salsa with cherry tomatoes and the tiny "mouthfuls" of fresh mozzarella called bocconcini. *Toss the salsa with cold pasta, serve it over mixed greens, or spoon it onto grilled slices of country bread.*

Makes about 3 cups

2 cups red and/or yellow cherry tomatoes, halved

1 cup bocconcini, cut in halves

2 tablespoons chopped basil, mint, or cilantro

2 tablespoons balsamic vinegar

$^1/_3$ cup extra-virgin olive oil

Salt

In a bowl, toss the tomatoes with the *bocconcini*, herbs (basil, mint, or cilantro), vinegar, and oil. Season to taste with salt.

Japanese Cucumber Salsa

xxxxx

Sunomono *is a Japanese salad made with sliced cucumbers in a tangy dressing; you may have seen it on the menu at your favorite sushi restaurant. If you dice the cucumbers, sunomono becomes a salsa that makes a lively accompaniment to fresh oysters, seared tuna steaks, or fried soft-shell crabs. Feel free to experiment with this simple recipe, adding shreds of dried seaweed, toasted sesame seeds, or crushed red chile flakes.*

Makes about 2 cups

2 small cucumbers, peeled, seeded, and diced (2 cups)

3 tablespoons rice wine vinegar

1 tablespoon sugar

Salt

In a bowl, toss the cucumbers with the rice wine vinegar and sugar. Add salt to taste. Marinate the salad for at least 20 minutes. Taste again, adjust the salt and sugar, if necessary, and serve.

Black Bean Salsa

xxxxx

Makes about 3 cups

1 can (15 ounces) black beans, rinsed and drained

1/2 red bell pepper, stemmed, seeded, and finely diced

1/2 yellow bell pepper, stemmed, seeded, and finely diced

2 jalapeño chiles, stemmed, seeded, and minced

1/2 medium yellow onion, finely diced

2 cloves garlic, minced

1/4 cup chopped cilantro

2 tablespoons olive oil

Juice of 2 limes

Salt

When I was a pantry cook at a big hotel in Albuquerque, I used to make this salad for our lunch buffet. At the hotel I made it in five-gallon batches, but here I've scaled it down a bit for you. Serve it as a side dish, over grilled meats, or simply with chips.

In a large bowl, toss the black beans with the red and yellow bell peppers, jalapeños, onion, garlic, cilantro, olive oil, and lime juice. Season to taste with salt.

Kachumber

xxxxxx

This condiment from India is nearly identical to a Mexican salsa, and it performs a similar role in the Indian meal, providing a fresh, light contrast to the rich intensity of curries.

In a bowl, toss the cucumber with the tomatoes, onion, chile, cilantro, and lime. Season to taste with salt and serve.

Makes about 2½ cups

1 small cucumber, peeled, seeded, and finely diced

2 medium tomatoes, seeded and finely diced

½ red onion, finely diced

1 serrano chile, stemmed, seeded, and minced

2 tablespoons minced cilantro leaves

Juice of 1 lime

Salt

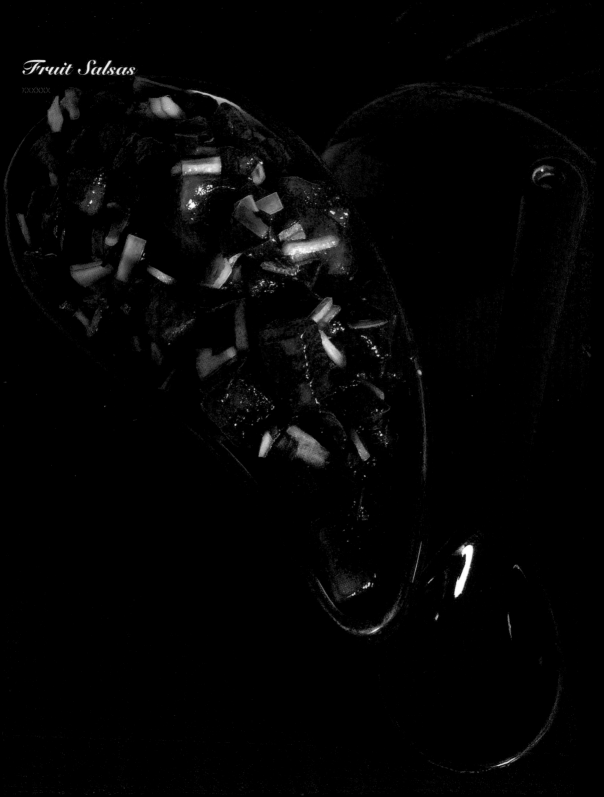

Watermelon and Basil Salsa

xxxxxx

Use a seedless watermelon, if you can find one, and you'll save yourself a little hassle making this salsa. If you have pink and yellow watermelons you can use some of each for a prettier result. I like the combination of basil and watermelon, but you can also use cilantro or mint. Serve it over any kind of fish or seafood.

In a bowl, toss the watermelon with the onion, chile, basil leaves, and lime juice. Season to taste with salt.

Makes about 2 cups

1 1/2 cups diced watermelon (seeds removed)

1/4 cup diced red onion

1 serrano chile, seeded and minced

10 basil leaves, shredded

Juice of 1 lime

Salt

Habanero Peach Salsa with Fresh Ginger

xxxxx

Makes about 1½ cups

2 ripe, but firm, peaches

½ cup diced red onion

¼ habanero chile, minced

½ teaspoon grated
fresh ginger root

Salt

The ginger in this salsa adds pleasant depth and complexity to the sweetness of the fruit and the fire of the chile. It is excellent served with salty tortilla chips, red chile- and pork-filled tamales, or roasted chicken. If you can't find fresh habaneros, substitute a little bit of crushed chile pequín or another kind of crushed red chile rather than a fresh green chile. If you find nice, ripe nectarines you can substitute them for the peaches and avoid the hassle of peeling them.

Bring 2 quarts of water to a boil in a medium saucepan. Slice a shallow 1½-inch-long "x" in the base of each peach. Gently add the peaches to the pot of boiling water and cook about 30 seconds, just long enough to loosen the skins. Use a slotted spoon to transfer the peaches to a plate. When the peaches are cool enough to handle, peel the skins off, starting from the "x" at the bottom, and dice the fruit into ½-inch cubes.

In a bowl, toss the peaches with the onion, chile, and ginger. Allow the salsa to rest 30 minutes, giving time for the flavors to meld and the chile heat to calm, then add salt to taste.

Grilled Peach Salsa with Rosemary

These grilled peaches partner beautifully with grilled chicken or pork, but they're exciting enough to serve as a side dish, too.

Preheat a gas or charcoal grill to medium-low.

Brush the cut sides of the peach halves and both sides of the onions with olive oil. Grill about 5 minutes on each side. Transfer the onions and peaches to a cutting board and slice the peach halves into 4 to 6 pieces. Cut the onion rings in half, making half-moon shaped pieces. Toss the peaches and onions with the rosemary, lemon juice, and chile Caribe. Salt to taste. Allow the salsa to rest 20 minutes before serving.

Makes about 3 cups

3 ripe, but firm, peaches, pitted and halved

$1/2$ red onion, sliced into rings 1 inch thick

Olive oil

1 tablespoon chopped rosemary

1 tablespoon lemon juice

1 tablespoon chile Caribe (optional)

Salt

Fennel and Grapefruit Pico de Gallo

xxxxxx

Makes about 2½ cups

2 medium pink grapefruits

1 medium bulb of fennel

4 mild yellow chiles, 1–2 jalapeño chiles, or ¼ habanero chile, stemmed, seeded, and minced

2 shallots, minced

Salt

My best recipe inspirations come to me in the first few moments after waking. Some Mexican pico de gallos contain crunchy jicama and sweet oranges; this puts sweet, crunchy fennel together with tangy pink grapefruit. The result is a totally untraditional flavor that is true to the fresh, crisp nature of pico. Serve it with grilled fish or toss it with chopped cooked shrimp for a refreshing first course.

Segment the grapefruits. Slice away all of the peel and pith from the fruits, then use a paring knife to cut the grapefruit segments away from the membrane that separates them. Cut each segment into about 5 smaller pieces.

Slice 1 inch from the bottom of the fennel bulb and discard it. Remove the feathery stems and save them for garnish. Slice off the top 3 inches of stem and discard them. Dice the remaining fennel into pieces about the same size as the grapefruit pieces.

In a bowl, toss together the grapefruit, fennel, minced chiles, and shallots. Season to taste with salt.

Mango Pomegranate Salsa

xxxxxx

Ruby red pomegranate seeds make this salsa stunningly beautiful. Serve it with chips or toss it with strips of grilled chicken and serve over a bed of lettuce.

Peel the pomegranate and separate the seeds from the pith. (If you do this in a bowl of water, the pith will float and the seeds will sink.) Measure out about ½ cup of seeds.

In a bowl, toss the pomegranate seeds with the mango, onion, jalapeño, mint, and lime juice. Season to taste with salt and serve.

Makes about 2 cups

1 medium pomegranate

1 large mango, peeled, seeded, and diced

¼ cup diced white onion

1 jalapeño chile, stemmed, seeded, and minced

2 tablespoons chopped mint leaves

Juice of 1 lime

Salt

Cranberry Pineapple Salsa

xxxxxx

Makes about 2 cups

Leftover turkey breast is a lot more exciting served with this cranberry salsa.

1 cup diced pineapple

¹/₂ cup dried cranberries

¹/₄ cup diced red onion

2 serrano chiles, seeded and minced

1 tablespoon lemon juice

1 tablespoon lime juice

Salt

¹/₄ cup chopped fresh cilantro leaves

In a bowl, toss the pineapple with the cranberries, onion, chiles, and lemon and lime juices. Season to taste with salt, then cover and allow to rest for at least 1 hour. Stir in cilantro and serve.

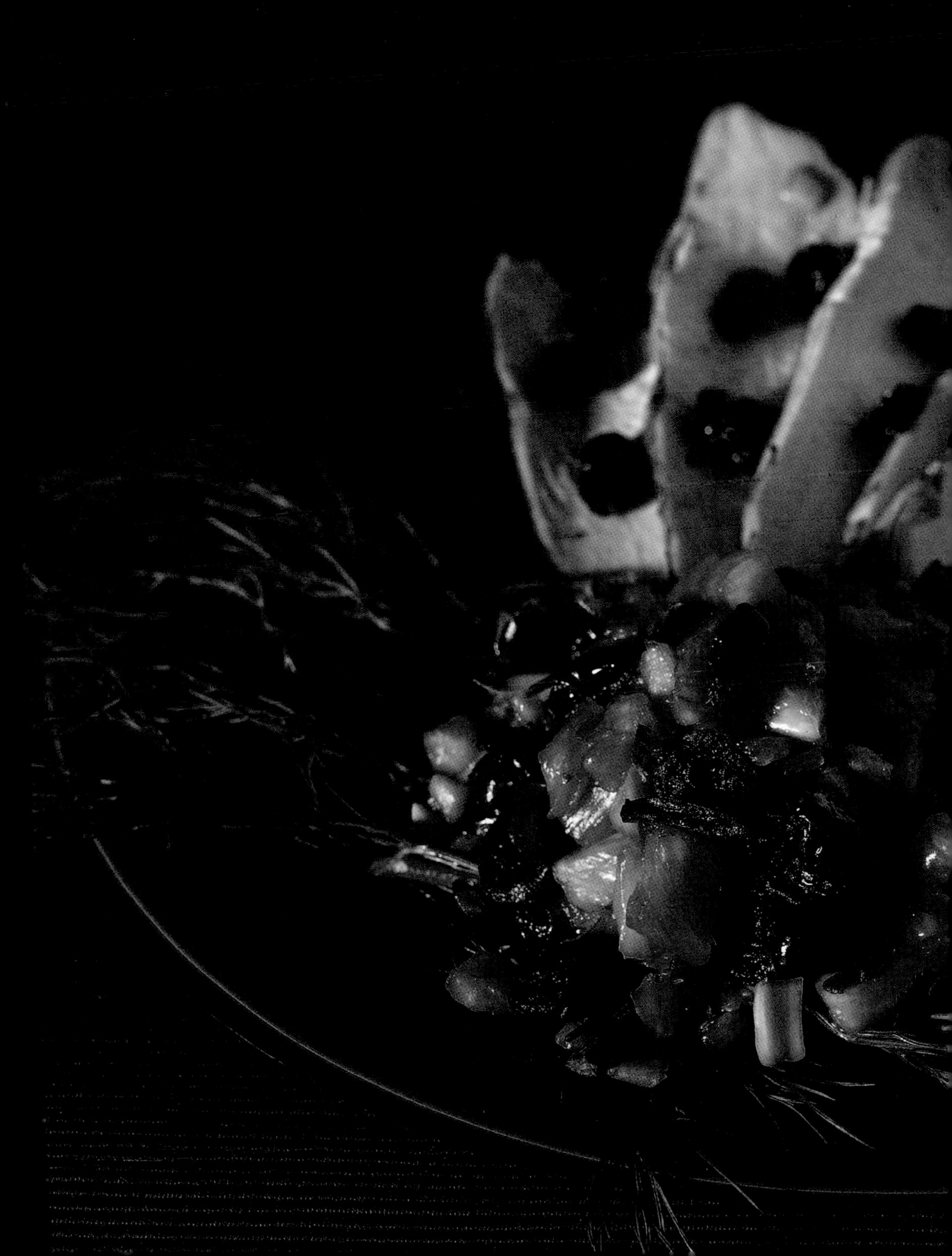

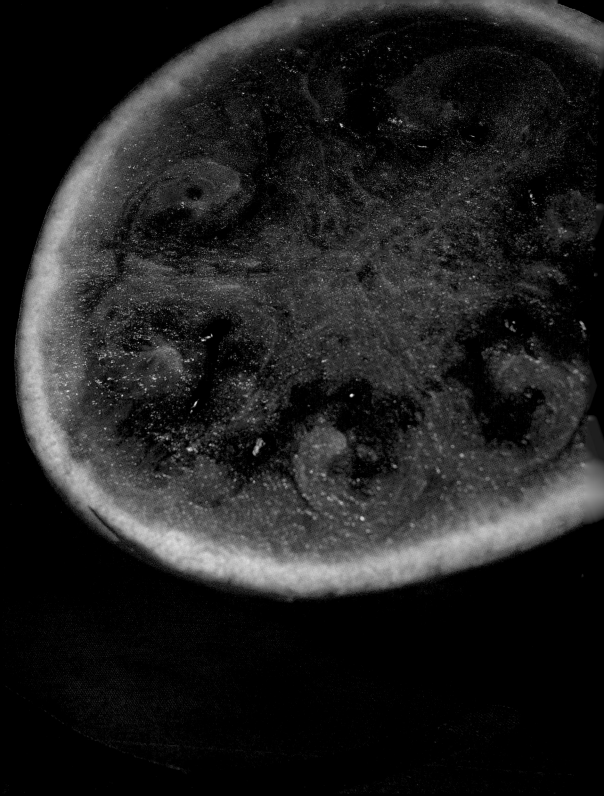

Watermelon and Jicama Pico de Gallo

xxxxxx

Nothing could be further from jarred commercial salsa than this incredibly crisp, crunchy, fresh combination of fruit and jicama.

Segment the orange. Slice away all of the peel and pith from the orange, then use a paring knife to cut the individual segments away from the membrane that separates them. Cut each segment into about 5 smaller pieces. You should have about ½ cup.

In a bowl, toss the orange segments with the watermelon, jicama, jalapeño, cilantro, and lime juice. Season to taste with salt.

Makes about 2½ cups

1 small orange

1 cup diced, seeded watermelon

¹/₂ cup diced jicama

1 jalapeño chile, stemmed, seeded, and minced

2 tablespoons chopped cilantro leaves

Juice of 1 lime

Salt

Summer Cherry Salsa

xxxxxx

Makes about 2 cups

1 pound cherries, pitted and chopped

2 tablespoons finely chopped red onion

1 serrano chile, seeded and chopped

2 tablespoons chopped cilantro leaves

2 teaspoons lime juice

2 teaspoons lemon juice

Salt

This salsa will be sweetest if you use Bing cherries, but it's even more interesting when you use a combination of Bing, Rainier, and sour cherries. You can use a cherry pitter, but if the cherries are really ripe it's often faster to just squish them between your fingers—the pit pops right out. Try making burritos or tacos with slices of roast pork and this salsa. It's also good warmed up and served over grilled salmon or pan-seared duck breast.

In a bowl, toss the cherries with the onion, chile, cilantro, and lime and lemon juices. Season to taste with salt and serve.

Jamaican Orange Salsa

xxxxxx

This Caribbean-inspired condiment gets its unusual flavor from allspice, which is native to the West Indies and produced in great quantities in Jamaica. Serve it with grilled seafood.

Slice away all of the peel and pith from the orange, remove the seeds, then finely chop it. In a bowl, toss the orange, habanero, onion, cilantro, olive oil, and allspice. Season to taste with salt, then allow to rest 30 minutes. Taste again, adjust the seasonings, and serve.

Makes about 1 ½ cups

1 orange

$1/4$ habanero chile, stemmed, seeded, and minced

$1/2$ red onion, diced

$1/4$ cup chopped cilantro leaves

2–3 tablespoons olive oil

$1/2$ teaspoon freshly ground allspice

Salt

Apricot and Lavender Salsa

xxxxxx

Makes about 2 cups

1/2 **pound ripe apricots, pitted and chopped**

1/4 **cup diced red onion**

1/4 **habanero chile, stemmed, seeded, and chopped**

1 **teaspoon dried lavender**

1–2 **tablespoons lemon juice**

Salt

It may sound strange, but apricots and lavender taste great together, both exuding the flavor of summer. Try this salsa over thick slices of pork loin or shrimp tacos. Be careful not to overdo the habanero here; it's supposed to give just a little heat in the background, not send steam shooting out your ears. Look for dried lavender in the bulk herbs section of your natural foods store.

In a bowl, toss the apricots with the onion, habanero, lavender, and lemon juice. Allow the mixture to rest for at least 30 minutes, then add salt to taste, and more chile or lavender if desired.

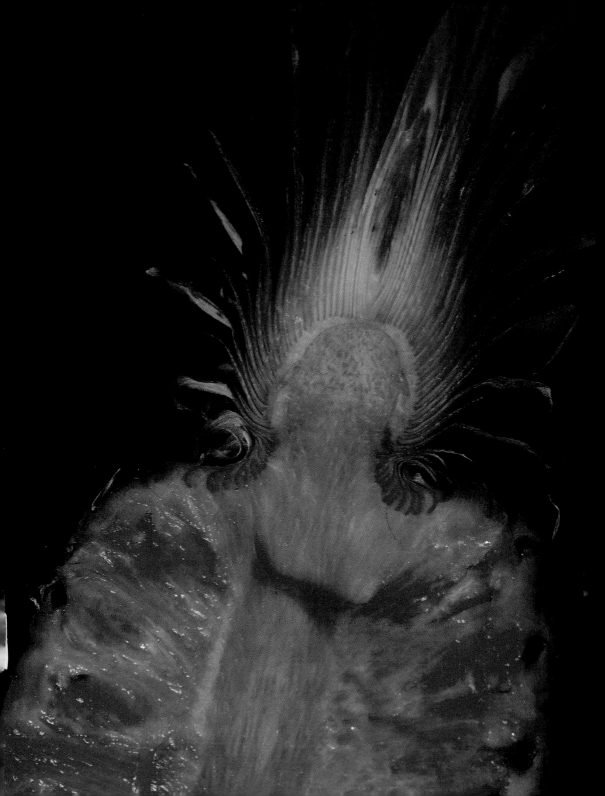

Grilled Pineapple Salsa with Chipotle and Mint

xxxxxx

The sweetness of the pineapple is brought out with a little bit of honey, and the smoky chipotle is contrasted against the bright mint. Try this salsa with thick slices of ham, leg of lamb, or just tacos.

Preheat a gas or charcoal grill to medium.

Using a heavy knife, trim the top and bottom from the pineapple and quarter it. Lightly brush the pineapple and onion pieces with oil. Grill about 5 minutes per side. Remove from the heat and allow to cool.

Trim the bumpy outer skin and tough core from the pineapple wedges. Chop the grilled fruit into bite-sized pieces. Dice the grilled onion.

In a large bowl, stir together the adobo sauce, honey, and lime juice. Add the onion, 2½ cups of the pineapple, and the mint. Season to taste with salt and serve.

Makes about 3 cups

1 fresh pineapple

½ red onion, sliced into rings 1 inch thick

Olive oil

2 tablespoons sauce from a can of chipotles in adobo

2 tablespoons honey

Juice of 1 lime

¼ cup chopped mint leaves

Salt

Fiery Tropical Fruit Salsa

xxxxxx

Makes about 2 cups

¹/₂ cup diced papaya

¹/₂ cup diced fresh pineapple

¹/₂ cup diced kiwifruit

¹/₄ cup diced red, green, or yellow bell pepper

¹/₄ cup diced red onion

¹/₂ (or more) habanero chile, seeds and stems removed, minced

2 tablespoons orange juice, fresh preferred

1 tablespoon lime juice, fresh preferred

2 tablespoons minced fresh cilantro leaves

Salt

Feel free to improvise with the combination of tropical fruits for this colorful salsa. The fruity, floral, and—yes—fiery flavor of the habanero chile is perfect here. Be warned that habaneros are hottest right after they've been cut, so the flavor will mellow significantly as the salsa rests.

In a large bowl, combine the papaya, pineapple, kiwifruit, bell pepper, onion, and chile. Add the orange and lime juices and the cilantro and toss to combine. Season to taste with salt.

SOURCES

www.melissaguerra.com
A great selection of dried chiles, herbs, spices, and more.

www.mexgrocer.com
Ingredients as well as molcajetes and tejolotes, tortilla presses, comals,
and packaged Mexican grocery items.

www.loschileros.com
A New Mexico–based company that sells dried chiles, blue corn, and other items.

www.gourmetsleuth.com
A wide range of Mexican ingredients, plus molcajetes and tejolotes and
helpful information.

www.herbsofmexico.com
A huge selection of herbs and teas.

www.penzeys.com
Spices, spices, and more spices. Plus some chiles.

www.adrianascaravan.com
An excellent source for hard-to-find chiles and other
ingredients.

INDEX